SCHUYLER SPIRITUAL SERIES
VOL. 7

7426

PRAYER
AND
SELF-KNOWLEDGE

Anselm Grün, O.S.B.

BMH Publications

Benedictine Mission House
P.O.Box 528
Schuyler, Nebraska 68661-0528

Original Title
Gebet und Selbsterkenntnis
Anselm Grün, OSB
© Vier - Türme - Verlag, Münsterschwarzach,1979
ISSN 0171-6360
ISBN 3-87868-105-4

First English Edition:
Translated by Sr. M. Francis De Sales Market, OSB
Edited by Edgar Friedmann
St. Paul Publications, Makti, Philippines
ISBN 971-504-061-6

US Revised Edition
Copyright © 1993 by BMH Publications
All rights reserved.
ISBN 1-56788-009-6

PRAYER
AND
SELF-KNOWLEDGE

Anselm Grün

CONTENTS

INTRODUCTION

Spiritual direction today has increasingly become the domain of psychology. Psychologists tell us what is good for the human soul, for the human "psyche" of humanity, and what will do it harm. Theologians, for their part, seem to have lost confidence in their own experience with spiritual direction and are trying to adopt psychological methods – sometimes very uncritically – for the guidance of souls. It is true, of course, that spiritual directors can no longer bypass the findings of psychology. But instead of looking to psychology for every notion of health and well-being, instead of measuring theology by the norms of psychology – sometimes even subordinating it – it would be far healthier for people of our time to consider the psychological insights issuing from the practice of religion. A theology that caters to the most varied schools of psychology will never be taken seriously by professionals in the field. Psychologists today expect theologians to bring to the open, for the sake of their contemporaries, all the rich discoveries which people of every age have garnered through their prayer.

The practice of prayer which we find among the monastics of the third to sixth centuries is a treasure-trove for psychological research. For the Ancients, the ways of religion and psychology were not yet distinct. The purely religious way was at the same time the psychological way. The religious way incorporated many of the psychological insights and methods which today's science, so intent on being independent, would claim for its own. The ancient monastics found in prayer the source of self-knowledge and a remedy for most of the wounds which today we seek to heal with one program or other of psychotherapy.

Prayer has both an analytic and a therapeutic function. In prayer, a person comes to recognize his evil inclinations and infirmities, and there also will find healing. The one who prays is not simply pious, but through prayer becomes more mature: a healthier, wiser, more vibrant person; a person who, in today's jargon, has "sorted oneself out," has become identified with the self, has attained self-realization.

The self-realization which we strive to attain through numerous psychological and meditative practices was, for the Christian monastics of old, the result of a regime of prayer which they intensely pursued. Self-realization was not per se their goal. The monastic ideal was not so much to exalt and actualize the self, but rather to seek God.

In turning toward the ideal of self-realization, the modern child of Adam and Eve is at center stage. Everything revolves around the individual. Even God is recruited for my purposes. Thus meditation and the practice of religion have taken for their object the development of all my human faculties. Having learned that the religious element is also part of our wholeness, that too must be developed. In this scenario, God becomes a means to an end, not interesting for God's own sake, but only as an agent of my self-fulfillment.

The monastics, on the other hand, were not so self-centered; they were seeking only God. They tried to clear out from their inner being all obstacles to union with God. In doing so, they soon found out that God is beyond our reach unless we stop overlooking these things and begin to know ourselves as we really are. We come to God-knowledge only through self-knowledge.

This was already pointed out by the first significant monastic writer, Evagrius Ponticus (†399):

> "If you want to know God, then first learn to know yourself."[1]

Clement of Alexandria (†211) had proposed, long before Evagrius, that self-knowledge is the basis of God-knowledge:

> "It would seem, now as always, that to know oneself is the greatest lesson, for to know oneself is also to know God."[2]

In the same vein, Nilus of Syria (†ca. 430) wrote in a letter to a young monastic:

> "Before all else, know yourself. Nothing is more difficult, more toilsome, more de-

manding of hard work. But when you have come to know yourself, you will also be able to know and come close to God."[3]

The self-evaluation which these monastics had in mind has two different aspects. On the one hand, we know ourselves in terms of God's greatness, which is mirrored in us because every human being is created as an image of God. This understanding of human self-knowledge we find above all in the writings of Origen and Ambrose and then also, under their influence, in the monastic writers of the middle ages.

William of St. Thierry (†1148) commenting on the Song of Songs, represents this viewpoint and speaks in the name of God:

"Know yourself, because you are my image, and so you will come to know me, whose image you are. In finding yourself, you will find me."[4]

But on the other hand, according to Bernard of Clairvaux (†1153), we must acknowledge that our likeness to God has been disfigured.

"You were modeled upon the image and likeness of God. But if you have lost that likeness and become like the brute animals, you nevertheless retain the image. If, having been exalted to the heights, you did not at the same time acknowledge the mire of which you were made, then by all means do not sink deeper into the mire. Recognize, instead, that you are still an image of God and blush for shame that you have covered it over with a foreign likeness. Think of your dignity and be filled with remorse for having so degraded it. Never lose sight of your beauty so that you may shudder the more at your ugliness."[5]

The monastics of the third century to the sixth had emphasized more the aspect of human wretchedness, which one who truly acquires self-knowledge can hardly ignore. Self-knowledge is the path to humility, and on this path one encounters oneself as a sinner who has been straying far away from God.

A brother approached the Abba Sisois and said: "I notice in my mind that the thought of God is ever present." The old man replied: "This is no great deal to be occupied with the thought of God. To see yourself as the lowest of all creatures is great indeed. That, together with bodily toil, will draw you to humility."[6]

Antony the Great (†356), whom tradition has called 'the Father of monastics', was of the same opinion:

Abba Antony said to Abba Poimen: "Humanities greatest work is to accept the guilt of their sins in the eyes of God and to expect temptations till their final breath."[7]

Both aspects pertain to self-knowledge. Each and every one of us is an image of God. We should try to appreciate the dignity, the beauty, the goodness which God has implanted in us, the capacity we have to become God's dwelling place. At the same time we should be rid of everything that hides or distorts this image. We should uncover all the darkness, the evil, the deception, the diabolical rot that lies within us. Thereupon God will heal us, restore the image originally made, and let us become what is to be intended for us. This is nothing else than self-realization. We develop more clearly as the image of God; or, rather, God's image is developed in us.

For the ascetics of earlier times – men and women both, living alone in the desert, then later in monasteries – the path toward self-realization was always the path of prayer.

Chapter I

PRAYER: A SOURCE OF SELF-KNOWLEDGE

a) Prayer impels us to Self-encounter

The monastic ideal of prayer is to speak with God, and to turn the affections of one's heart to God. But we discover time and again that, in prayer, God wants us to reflect first on our condition and our heart's desires. St. Augustine writes how God repeatedly did this to him.

> "But you, O Lord, while he [Ponticianus] was speaking, turned me around to face myself, taking me from behind my back, where I had placed myself in hiding because I was unwilling to look at myself. You set me in front of my own face, that I might see how ugly I was, how deformed and defiled, how covered with spots and sores. I looked and was horrified. But there was no place I could flee from so wretched a spectacle."[8]

In prayer we cannot flee, for God does not allow to be misused as a means of escape. This God proves to us when during prayer, God allows our thoughts and feelings to rise to the surface, where the interior condition of our soul becomes much more apparent. Abba Nilus warned his disciples:

> "Everything you do in revenge against a brother who has offended you will rise up in your heart at the hour of prayer."[9]

Another of the Ancients held as worthless all prayer that does not confront us with our true self:

> "If we, while praying, do not keep our deeds in mind we try to pray in a vacuum."[10]

It is therefore a fact of experience that prayer impels us to self-encounter. The monastics of old gave the following reason for this: as soon as one begins to pray, the demons become jealous and try to subvert the process by stirring up evil thoughts, passions, and emotions. One should not be surprised at this but regard it as normal, indeed, should even expect it, as Evagrius advises:

> "If you have prayed, as is proper, expect what is not proper, and bravely hold your ground."[11]

When thoughts and passionate appetites distract us in prayer, there is little left for us to do but to stop praying and first come to grips with these intrusions.

William of St. Thierry (†1148) writes a graphic description of how, as soon as he begins to pray, a torrent of thoughts invades his mind. He doesn't try to suppress them or thrust them aside, but deliberately confronts them. He meets them head-on, believing that this is the only way to get rid of the disturbance.

In Chapter IX of his *Meditations* he writes:

> "And so, leaving my gift before the altar and driven — almost shaken — by the need to examine my inner self, I kindle the lamp of the Word of God. With this in hand and a spirit of grim determination, I proceed to the dark house of my conscience, for I mean to discover once and for all whence these shadows and hideous vapors arise that would separate me from the Light of my heart.
>
> But what should happen then? A swarm of gnats appears, and erupts before my eyes; it almost drives me back! I enter, all the same, into a house which is mine by right. Next, a cloud of thoughts comes up to greet me! — so bold, so disjointed, so random and confused, that the heart of the person who begot them is unable to sort them out! Undaunted, I take a seat, as if to be their judge. I order them to stand before me, so that I can look at all their faces and determine what each thought contains, for I intend to assign to each one its proper place within my house."[12]

Having dissipated the fog — for awhile at least — [by passing sentence under the broad categories of 'unclean', 'idle', and 'busy'], William decides to look below, to the region where his thoughts originate: in the moods, feelings, and emotions. He wants to bring order to that level, too, because he knows that thoughts are produced by feelings; it is only when feelings like ambition, anger, hatred, and petty annoyance are superseded by love, that his thoughts will finally come to rest and he can turn his attention back to God.

> "Now that the dank and dismal fog is cleared away, I am able to gaze with sounder sight upon you, O Light of Truth. Everything else is kept away, and I can lock myself in company with you, O Truth, and hide in the loving shadow of your face. I can speak with you more intimately now, in a more familiar way. All the corners of my conscience, both deep and far, I shall openly reveal."[13]

Thus monastics [but, in reality, everyone] at prayer need to observe themselves reflexively, that is, by monitoring the thoughts and moods that occur to them and by probing into their cause. Self-knowledge, however, is more a means than a valid purpose: it helps toward better prayer. Through self-knowledge, everything that tends to disturb or hinder prayer should be removed. The monastics cannot simply shake off or suppress the thoughts and moody feelings that take hold of them and prevent them from prayer; they can gain release only if they boldly confront them and bring them to the ground. When monastics and spiritual writers of times past called repeatedly for strict self-observation and self-knowledge, they set before their eyes the goal of enabling a kind of contemplative prayer that is true and genuine.

St. Antony considered it essential to a monastic vocation that he or she knows him/herself:

> "It does us great good to withdraw into our cell and during this life to ponder our condition, until we know what kind of person we are."[14]

St. Gregory, in Book 2 of his *Dialogues*, writes of young St. Benedict:

> "He kept a close watch over his life and actions. While searching continually into his own soul, he always placed himself in the presence of his Creator. This kept his mind's eye from straying to things outside."[15]

The Philokalia, a collection of writings on the Jesus Prayer, expressly defines the object of self-examination:

> "The more you direct your awareness to your thoughts, the better you will be able to call upon Jesus with ardent longing."[16]

Self-knowledge is a pre-requisite for prayer:

> "It is indispensable for a life of prayer to truly discover one's emotions and tendencies, as well as to keep careful watch over all external influences."[17]

Prayer forces us to self-knowledge because we cannot pray with recollection without knowing our innermost thoughts and strivings. Without interior vigilance, our prayer will be constantly plagued with distractions.

On the other hand, the distractions which continually interrupt our prayer are a good opportunity for self-knowledge. J. Hausherr, one of the best-informed experts on ancient monasticism, believes that distractions at prayer have the same function as dreams:

> "Distractions are extremely valuable because they give us directions. They are a kind of wakeful dream about the matters that occupy us."[18]

As dreams give us information about what is going on in the unconscious depths of our soul, so also with distractions, which, likewise, spring from the unconscious. They reveal the tendencies of our heart. When we take notice that we repeatedly think of the same matters, of certain people or events, or that the same problems and plans swirl around in our heads, we can draw very valuable conclusions about ourselves. And as soon as we have come to know ourselves better in this way, distractions will decrease and we will become able to pray to God with quiet recollection.

2. *Prayer as an aid toward Self-knowledge*

Self-knowledge is not only a prerequisite for prayer, but, reciprocally, prayer helps us to know ourselves.

> "Nothing more deeply penetrates the heart than prayer. When we pray we enter into the holy presence of God and are enlightened to our very core. Everything is revealed."[19]

Prayer stations me directly in the presence of God whose light reaches beyond the facade of my doing and thinking. It allows me to know the true motives of my actions and to discover the reasons for my thoughts and moods. According to the Philokalia, it is only the Holy Spirit who makes real self-knowledge possible.

> "The Holy Spirit alone bestows true self-knowledge: without the Spirit not even the most astute person can properly know or become aware of this inmost spiritual condition."[20]

Many a thing I would never discover in myself without prayer. For it is precisely through confrontation with God that I become aware of what's wrong with me. Prayer discloses what self-analysis could never figure out.

> "The Jesus Prayer possesses the virtue of calling forth the hidden passions lodged in our

heart, of opening up the confinement in which the tempter binds us."[21]

The ability of prayer to lead us to a deeper self-knowledge consists in the fact that it confronts us with a person, with the Living God. Prayer is not monologue, not self-contemplation but conversation, a meeting with a person distinct from myself. This enables me to take a stand outside myself, from which I can see myself more objectively and comprehensively than when, by mere self-observation, I revolve about myself and never break loose.

The person who looks only at oneself is blind to many aspects of one's being; whereas in prayer, from myself toward God, I can see myself from God's point of view and know myself far better in God's light.

From the realm of psychology, C.G. Jung thus describes the positive function of prayer for human self-knowledge, claiming that

> "prayer places a person in the duality of the I and the "divine you". This duality enables a person to break out of one's own little ego, to see oneself from another vantage point."[22]

Normally, we live all too much on the conscious level. Prayer allows the unconscious also to have a voice. Jung calls prayer a

> "dialogue with one's unconscious self, which thereby is enabled to reveal its helpful powers

and precipitate a process of spiritual transformation and healing."[23]

Prayer helps a person venture forth from the little ego which is imprisoned in one's consciousness, to encounter the self, our actual core, which unites the conscious and the unconscious, divine and human. This, says C. G. Jung, is necessary for the process of self-realization, individuation.

Self-knowledge meant more to the monastics than getting to know the unknown, and more than perceiving one's unique dark spots. Self-knowledge certainly included acknowledgment of their own sins. In the light which comes from God I realize that I am a sinner; I discover in myself whatever is opposed and whatever shuts me off from God.

The Philokalia differentiates between self-knowledge resulting from prayer and natural self-knowledge. In natural self-knowledge, I take stock of my limitations, for by nature the human person is able to distinguish good from evil. Yet, on the account of my fallen nature, I can detect only the major faults. Through interior prayer however, the perception of one's own reality is better focused.

"Spiritual self-examination, which takes place in the presence of God, reveals things that have been concealed to a degree hitherto never suspected... It opens your eyes and lets you see clearly the condition of your soul. On this point the Ancients present an eloquent analogy: The conscience of a person who lives on

21

an external level is like muddy water; at the bottom there are the swarms of evil: worms, snakes, and crocodiles. One suspects and knows nothing of this, for the muddy water prevents from seeing clearly. So one lives a carefree life, considers oneself a good person, and passes judgment on others. The conscience of an enlightened person, on the contrary, is like clean water. In the sunlight of God's grace, every speck becomes visible, and every little shadow grieves one deeply, because it separates from God. True self-knowledge is a clean awareness of one's own faults and failings, to such a degree that they fill up everything. A painful self-knowledge, permeated with contrition, accompanies all real prayer."[24]

Acknowledgment of one's sins is genuine only when one suffers on their account. Thus the Philokalia speaks repeatedly of painful self-knowledge, which must be accompanied by deep contrition: "True, moving contrition,"[25] in the words of the Philokalia, produces a deep interior humility, which is necessary for genuine prayer. It alone will purify the heart and keep the one who is praying from pride and self-elation. Prayer is not a means to be employed for self-interest or out of mere curiosity. Much more, it is concerned with keeping a person in the right attitude toward God and with that humility to which an unsparing and unrestricted self-knowledge leads.

3. *Prayer as a method of Self-knowledge*

The monastics developed forms and methods of prayer and meditation which support the process of self-knowledge. Thus prayer itself became an outstanding means of self-knowledge. The examination of thoughts, which the Ancients call for ever and again, takes place neither before nor after prayer, but in and through prayer. So the art of intelligible prayer

> consists precisely in placing the intellect in watchful emptiness over the heart, to control all kinds of temptations, to see how, when and whence and in what dimensions they approach."[26]

Thus self-observation is already prayer. Inasmuch as we reflect on ourselves and let our thoughts be questioned by God, we pray.

Evagrius is also of this opinion, when he counsels monastics on prayer:

> They should observe their thoughts, take note of their duration, their coming and going, their relationship to each other; their times, and which demons they activate. Then, which demon follows which, and which does not accompany another one. And they should ask Christ to enable them to discover their cause and their basis."[27]

In conversation with Christ, that is, in prayer we should discover the sources and the background of our thoughts. This conversation with God about ourselves is not only a preparation for, but is already prayer. We are the topic of this conversation. We should speak to God about ourselves, should lay open our life to God, and ascertain from God the one great purpose of our life. If here, we ourselves become the subject of prayer, it certainly does not mean that God is being degraded as a means to human self-knowledge. Much more, the goal of prayer is the encounter with God. But in order that we may be able to meet God in our real condition, we must first of all lay open our thoughts and emotions before God and not fool ourselves. Not until we have realized in this conversation who we really are and in what condition we find ourselves, can a genuine confrontation take place, in which we do not hide behind a false mask, but lay ourselves open to God "skin-to-skin" without pious trappings.

Cassian, too, one of the most renowned monastic writers in the West, recognized forms of prayer in which monastics themselves are the theme of the prayer. Thus he says that monastics should keep daily before them in mediation the offenses they have received and should test themselves to see how they react. They should not deceive themselves but honestly be on their guard to see what feelings rise in their heart when they vividly confront the grievances, insults and injustices inflicted on them. They practically take the position of observers who, without evaluating, take note of what goes on within themselves. They are not impelled to this by any selfish motive – such as curiosity to know what transpires in their soul – but rather by the desire to place themselves in the position in which God wishes them to be: i.e., for monastics, in the disposition of humility and meekness.

Through reflection on insults and injuries the monastics should school themselves in patience and meekness. They should place themselves in such imaginary situations for as long a time as necessary to enable them to keep calm and cool, not only in meditation but also in reality. Self-knowledge is a means of healing and is in itself the first step toward healing. The more we recognize our faults and grieve over them in painful contrition, the sooner we will be healed of them.

Thus Cassian recommends that we

> purposely recall things that agitate us, so that, waging a constant war against them in our thoughts, we may the more quickly find the remedy."[28]

The method which Cassian here recommends has a striking resemblance to the active imagination which C. G. Jung has developed. Here one is concerned with making oneself more aware of unknown contents, either by further fantasizing a dream-picture or plunging oneself recklessly into a momentary situation to discern the emotion which caused it.[29] The purpose of this is to confront destructive affections and desires and to free oneself of all through the imagination. For Jung, too, such imagination can take place only in "religious," that is, "in reverent conscientious respect to the numinous."[30]

According to Cassian, the monastics should ever and again imagine themselves standing before God, under the judging and probing eye of God. Thus, they permit God to convict them of their perverse actions, their vices, their sins, and beg from God the strength to overcome their perversities; for they know that they cannot heal themselves, that no technique of meditation or prayer can effect their cure, but only the grace of God; to which they humbly submit themselves.

Self-knowledge comes not only from self-observation, but also in a decisive measure from observing our neighbors. Thus, praying for our neighbors is a fruitful means of self-knowledge; for while we pray for our neighbors, our relationship with them comes to light. In prayer for another, we renounce all effort of justifying ourselves; we seek to see the other in the light of God. In this light we see how we stand toward them. In an old adage, prayer for a neighbor who has offended me also becomes a means for me to recognize my own faults.[31] As soon as I stop seeing only the failings of others I become free to see myself and my own faults.

St. Benedict recommends praying with the newly-arrived guests before giving them the kiss of peace, "because of the delusions of the devil,"[32] which one can recognize only in prayer. Prayer helps me to recognize my judgments and the ground of my antipathies, and gives me an unbiased judgment of the value of the other.

Through prayer we discover that we are intimately bound with all humankind, and that the arrogance and evil we see in others is ingrained in our own selves. In praying for others we lose interest in blaming others; on the contrary, we become more and more aware that we ourselves are at fault when others behave as if everyone avoids and judges them.

Dostoyevsky has Starez Sossitna repeatedly proclaim the experience of the monastics that everyone is guilty before all and in all:

> "There is only one remedy: make yourself responsible for the sins of humanity. It is so in reality, friend, and as soon as you assume responsibility for all and for everything, you will see and recognize the fact that you are indeed responsible to all for everything."[33]

Whoever tries to see other people in the light of God as those whom God loves, will stop blaming their own faults and weaknesses on others. Prayer for others is an effective means to cease projecting guilt on others and to know one's own inner self. At the same time, prayer leads to a better knowledge of others, a knowledge that does not judge but understands to have compassion for others.

Another form of prayer that leads to self-knowledge is thanksgiving. Benedict repeatedly recommends this method in his Rule. His purpose is to clarify difficult situations to the monastics and to encourage them to give thanks for injuries and insults received. In giving thanks they will acknowledge God's designs and realize to what degree they are prepared to conform to the will of God.

Thus he says in Chapter 40 *Of the Measure of Drink:* that if there is no wine, the monastics should give thanks to God instead of asking why. The porter should meet each arriving guest with the greeting *Deo gratias,* regardless of whether the guest is appealing to the porter or not.[34] Only in this way will the porter be open to receive the other without prejudice.

In giving thanks, I try to accept everything in the way God gives it. While I thank God for all the happenings of my life, the unpleasant as well as the pleasant, for the good things as well as the bad, I accept myself with my past. And I can really acknowledge only what I have accepted. Not until I accept myself as one whom God so willed can I really know myself. Then I will discover what God's plans are in my regard; what image is intended to take form in me. The same is true of the many events and occurrences of my life. I will discover their true meaning only when I refrain from trying to get behind their meaning, and instead thank God for all the challenges I experience in my life.

In giving thanks I refrain from seeking my own solution and trust in God, who means it well. This trust leads to enlightenment, to a realization not of my own making or intelligence, but through grace. To thank for a misfortune which nearly ruins me... to thank for a brother or sister who riles me, seems silly. Yet, as soon as I begin to thank God for it, I realize how I resist God, how I try to manipulate God. In giving thanks I let go of self-made images of God and abandon myself to the true God, who will then reveal to me the truth about myself which often enough may be painful.

Chapter II

PRAYER AND COMPUNCTION OF HEART

The self-knowledge which prayer transmits to us must not be allowed to remain on the rational level; it must become realistic. The Philokalia speaks of the most painful kind of self-knowledge, a self-knowledge that goes to the heart, that reaches from the head to the heart and there causes pain. Thereby self-knowledge acquires another quality:

> "As long as the understanding lingered in the mind, this contemplation deviated to generalities. The heart, on the contrary, stirs up the extraordinary, which concerns us. Without any digression and excuses, it turns everything in us to the most effective aspect which grips us most deeply. We experience directly our own faults and weaknesses, as light compared with darkness."[35]

The Ancients speak here of compunction of heart, *compunctio cordis*, of grief (pathos) and of tears.[36] This theme, so vital to our Ancients for the spiritual life, seems to us at first sight unintelligible. Yet, it is worthwhile to explore this matter, for it is only in this way that we can rightly understand the self-knowledge which prayer indicates.

For monastics, self-knowledge is not a psychological knowledge of oneself; above all, it is not a curious discovery of psychological relationships about which one can then speak of cleverly and interestingly. Monastics do not look at themselves as an object which they wish to analyze; rather, in their endeavor at self-knowledge it is God whom they desire to discover and to encounter.

Self-knowledge is always knowledge of oneself before God, and this means: knowledge of one's sinfulness before God. Knowledge of one's sins comes appropriately neither before nor after the knowledge of God, but inasmuch as I know my sins, I also know God, and the moment I meet God, I am confronted with my sins. The self-knowledge in prayer can not be done objectively, made an object, but occurs in the encounter, and for this reason pierces the heart. I become painfully aware of my sins before God, in the presence of a person who loves me, who looks upon me with kindness.

The reaction to the awareness of one's sinfulness is sorrow, contrition, penance, weeping. The monastics of old repeatedly recommended weeping over one's sins and even continuing to weep long after one has received pardon. This sorrow and shedding of tears is not for particular sins and faults, but concerns me as a sinner, as a human being in whom sin dwells. The tears spring from sorrow over my separation from God, sorrow over a lost grace. Contrition is at the same time a longing for grace, for integrity, for harmony between body and soul, for peace, for the ability to give undivided love. This sorrow has nothing to do with sadness which the monastics numbered among the eight vices, nor with discouragement or depression, nor with pessimism or resignation. Sadness dries up the heart, robs it of elasticity, and makes it an empty void. Contrition, on the contrary, expresses itself in tears, in continued weeping over one's sins. Sadness paralyzes or disturbs; contrition makes fruitful and alive.

For Evagrius, it is a direct sign of *acedia* (sloth) to have a hardened soul which is unwilling to shed tears,[37] and he recommends begging for the gift of tears at the beginning of each prayer,

> "so that through sorrow you may soften what is hard in your soul."[38]

The monastics distinguish between different kinds of tears. There are childish tears, which we shed when we do not get what we want; there are tears of hurt feelings, of anxiety, tears of anger, of rage, of helplessness, and there are tears of self-pity. None of these tears can heal. On the contrary, they keep us bound to our faults, they establish us in our anger, in our hurt feelings, in our self-pity.

Cassian sets this kind of anger – "because of the anxieties of this life and its needs and tribulations, which oppress us," – in contrast to other kinds of weeping: a weeping which arises "when the sting of sin wounds our heart,"[39] which comes "from the contemplation of the eternal good things and the longing for the glory that is to come"; a weeping because of the fear of hell and a weeping over the hardness and blindness of others. When the monastics sing the praises of tears they mean above all weeping for one's own sins, which is almost identical with weeping out of longing for the salvation of God.

For Isaac of Nineve (5th century), tears are a sign that one has come close to the truth of things:

> "At the same time that grace began to open your eyes, so that you might see the true nature of things, your eyes began to shed tears which bathed your cheeks and the pressure of sinful desires was relieved in that they were peacefully locked up within yourself."[40]

And I. Hausherr points to the self-revealing function of tears:

> "Weeping is our way of coming closer to the truth, which is a divine attribute. Weeping means recognizing the truth about ourselves, even when it is not pleasing to us."[41]

Thus weeping is a sign that one has confronted the truth, that one has confronted oneself without trying to hide from oneself. Weeping possesses a special power of self-knowledge. "We shall weep... and understand everything,"[42] as Dostoyevsky expresses the fact that in weeping we discover the truth of things.

In weeping, I confront myself. Through weeping, everything suddenly becomes clear: my misery, my false motives and intentions, my malice, my evasiveness and my deep-seated egoism. The edifice of my virtue, so laboriously erected, collapses in my weeping. I get at all the false pretenses behind where I continuously try to hide my true self. While weeping, words fail me when I explain myself and my condition – words behind which I repeatedly hide myself. In weeping I confront myself unsparingly, at close range I experience myself without any medium over which I still have control. Even the thoughts to which I might still cling, vanish. Weeping is confrontation without mediation, without a go-between. In weeping, I let go of myself and abandon myself to the weeping which grasps me. Weeping becomes to me the only possible answer to an experience to which I no longer know how to respond. My body takes over and answers for me as I break into tears. My intellect and my spirit remain speechless.[43]

In weeping, as soon as all attempts at self-justification collapse and all masks are removed, the new person can appear, created in God's mercy, the whole being, for whom we long.

For Ephraim of Syria (†373), tears are the condition under which the new person can come forth:

"Through tears and through God's grace, the soul which was dead is resurrected."[44]

André Louf further describes this new person, who has crossed the threshold of contrition and has shed tears of sorrow over sin, which gently turns into tears of joy over the new-found life:

"From now on the person is completely at peace, after he or she, purely out of mercy, is destroyed and from the very beginning thoroughly restored again. One no longer recognizes oneself! The person has touched the abyss of sin and at the same moment, grasped the chasm of compassion and has learned how to break down before God, and cast off personal masks and weapons. Finally, one stands unarmed before the Creator, no longer making any attempt to defend oneself from God's love. The person is naked and bare; the virtues, the plans for becoming holy have been taken out of his or her hands. Toilsome, one only clings to one's misery to lay it open to mercy. God has become truly God, namely, the Redeemer of one's sins. Finally, the person even reconciles him or herself to this in order to rejoice in one's weakness. From now on perfection means nothing; before the eyes of God, it is but soiled clothing (Is. 64:5). The person's virtues are now only possessed in God; these are wounds, but through the mercy of God bound up and healed wounds. One can only give all the honor and glory to God, who works in him or her and unceasingly accomplishes wonders."[45]

In shedding tears, monastics weep not only over their sins, but at the same time, over the forgiveness they have received. They can no longer tell whether they are weeping more over themselves and their misery or over the love of God, which embraces them and lifts them out of their lowliness. In weeping they confront their own sinfulness, and also discover what grace is, what the love of God signifies: love for the unlovable, acceptance of the unacceptable. In weeping, the monastics lay themselves open not only to their sins but to the love of God. Their hearts react to God's love with tears. God's love penetrates and wounds their hearts to let the tears break forth. The weepers do not shut themselves off from God's love, but wounded by it, become capable to discover it.

Monastics again and again sing the praises of tears, which are at the same time tears of sorrow and of joy. They speak of the *charopoion penthos*, of joy-bringing sorrow. Tears dispel sadness and fear and produce a deep interior joy.

John Climacus (†600) says of tears:

> "Tears take away fear, and where there is no longer fear, the undimmed light of joy shines, and from this unfading joy springs forth the flower of the holy love of God"[46]

Peter Damiani (†1072) sings a never-ending hymn of praise: "*De laude lacrymarum* – the praise of tears."[47] Tears wash clean from

37

sin, wipe out the traces which sin has left in the soul, purify the heart. They are a bath for the soul, which not only purifies, but also refreshes and fills with pleasure. Tears fructify the soul, give it new life and bring deep interior peace. Painful and troublesome thoughts disappear. Tears protect from distractions and gather the spirit to pure prayer in God. Tears break down pride and drive away all thoughts to which a person might still proudly cling. They abandon the heart to the loving God and fill it with joy.

> "O spiritual delight of tears! Sweeter than honey and the honeycomb and nectar!"[48]

Thus Peter Damiani praises joy-bringing tears. Evagrius sees in tears a requisite for good prayer and for a real encounter with the true God. Without tears one does not encounter the true God, but just the images of one's own imagination. For Evagrius tears are a criterion for union with God:

> "If you believe it is not necessary to shed tears for your sins when you pray, remember that you withdraw yourself from God. Should you want to be forever bound to God, then shed burning tears."[49]

Whoever gives God access to oneself, who allows oneself to be overcome by God, breaks out in tears. In this Evagrius sees an important connection.

An Deum timeas, e lacrymis agnoscito! Whether you fear God, you will know by your tears.[50]

If you cannot weep, Evagrius tells us in this terse phrase, you need not imagine that you have experienced anything about God. Tears are a sign of the nearness of God, an expression of encounter with God, a bodily expression of the awareness of the nearness of a loving God. For Guigo the Carthusian, (†1137) tears are signs of God's arrival, signs and messengers of his consolations and joys.

"In these tears, recognize your Bridegroom, O Soul, and embrace Him. They are wonderful gifts and consolations which your Bridegroom gives you."[51]

Tears are, therefore, the human reaction to coming near God, a reaction which God calls forth so that we may experience the Creator.

H. Plessner, a Philosopher, one of the few who have dealt with the phenomenon of tears in recent years, describes tears as

"an emotion in its entirety to which a person surrenders without reserve, so that one no longer needs to answer from a distance."[52]

Decisive for tears is the lack of distance to the one who seizes and overcomes one.

To be moved

"is meeting with the issue itself, it is without intervention. Our relations and pro-

39

portionately urgent condition fall into an absolute end."[53]

In weeping, God touches me without the mediation of words or images; God touches my person. This shatters all manner of behavior over which I still have control and which I can dispose of at will. The only response that remains is capitulation, the abandonment of all that I have at my disposal. In tears I no longer wish to attain anything. I only abandon myself, to be touched, grasped. Tears here, however, are not the only criterion of whether I abandon myself without reserve to God or whether I am attached to my own reactions and wish to enjoy my own feelings. This way, I only confront myself again. The tears would not be genuine by the encounter with God, but self-produced for my interior enrichment.

Genuine tears are a gift of God's grace. They touch me, if God deigns to encounter me.

Tears have still another function for monastics. They unite body and soul. Sorrow springs precisely from the duality of body and soul, which breaks forth repeatedly in sin. Spirit and body, intellect and feeling, come in conflict because of sin. Maximus the Confessor (†662) says

> "that tears restore harmony between the higher and the lower senses, between intellect and feeling: they unite us with ourselves"[54]

Richard of St. Victor (†1173) is of the opinion that the struggle with tears is a sign of longing to realize the harmony between the interior and the exterior person.[55] Tears allow feelings to express themselves outwardly. They draw the body into the prayer. The person reacts to God's love no longer with mere thoughts, but with the whole being.

If tears have such a salutary effect, is there a means to call them forth, or do they remain a pure gift for which one can only wait in humility? Cassian does not favor one's wishing to break out in tears:

> "they would be unfruitful, forced, sickly forms of tears."[56]

Nilus counsels one who cannot weep to awaken the longing for tears within oneself and to give thanks for a brother or sister who is able to weep. Then one will receive a share of the other's gift.[57] Nilus holds that it is obviously justifiable to employ certain means to help bring forth tears. Thus he prescribes the following method to the Deacon Agapitos in answer to his question:

> "What should I do if I cannot weep with my bodily eyes?" – "You should recall how you have wept in a dream. Then you will also be able to weep when you are awake."[58]

Further counsel is given by an Ancient:

> "Weeping is an attitude, and they who desire this gift must devote much time to it, until

41

they have accustomed their spirit to meditate constantly on their sins and punishment, to think of the grave, and, in a word, to face it with all the fibers of their soul. They should meditate on how their forefathers spent their time, and where they are now. The Brother asked: 'And what about the monastics — should they think of their parents?' The sage answered: 'If you know that such thoughts will bring you to tears, then do so, and when the tears come, turn them in whatever direction you wish, whether it be your sins or another good train of thought. In fact, I know another brother who, when his heart was hard, beat himself several times and wept under the pain of the beating. Then he thought of his sins.'"[59]

Thus it is recommended here to call forth tears through natural means, through imaginations, which make one naturally weep. Then the tears should be turned away from the misconception that caused them and shed for one's own sins. Many people are brought to tears by watching a sad movie, by self-pity, or sentimental emotions. This is not the kind of weeping whose fruitful action the monastics praise. But one can turn this weeping upon oneself or one's sins, or direct it to God, and thus, it will become liberating, in which one can let go of oneself so that breaking out into tears washes away all hardness of heart and brings one nearer to God.

If we inquire into the actual significance of these seemingly strange thoughts of these ancient monastics with regard to weeping, we will discover several corrective measures for our own prayer. We are taught to restrain our tears as much as possible... yes, by all means to hide our feelings. This holds true not only for our social contacts with others but also in the religious sphere, in which, for fear of being considered sentimental, or having a piety based mainly on feelings, we prefer to withdraw to the rational level of meeting with God. Compunction of heart, weeping for one's sins, are expressions of that fact that I give in to my feelings, that I really take to heart the fact that I am a sinner. Mentally I can always shield myself from God and hide myself behind thoughts. But in weeping, all attempts at evasion break down, my masks fall away, I stand exposed before God and face my own nakedness. In giving in to my feelings by weeping I become capable of a better understanding of myself, of other people, of God.

> "Genuine insight is given only to a person who gives in to one's feelings. One who does not feel can understand neither oneself nor others."[60]

The feelings that break out in tears are to be distinguished from those violent emotions which, according to the teaching of Cassian, are signs that the roots of evil are still alive within. For Plessner, the difference between genuine and false emotions consists in the fact that genuine emotions are brought about by

43

an event or a person outside of oneself: i.e., through meeting with an "Other", with a "You", with "God".

> "In false emotions, the act of being spoken to is lacking in its objectivity and the person is permeated only by one's self-centered feelings."[61]

In false feelings, in the emotions which seize us, we simply gravitate around ourselves, taking pleasure in ourselves or passively allow ourselves to be permeated with sadness, irritation, anger. In these emotions, the personal self, the ego, which is disordered, which takes itself too seriously, always comes forward. Emotions render a person inwardly confused. On the contrary, weeping that gives in to genuine feelings leads one to interior peace and repose.

Climacus says that tears bestow

> "a complete, a blessed repose that exceeds all blissful movements of the spirit."[62]

In weeping, all my disquieting and confusing thoughts are put to rest. For in weeping I am not in my head, in which I will never find rest, but in my heart, which finds its inner peace in tears because it is allowed to express itself. Thus the discovery becomes plausible that after tears one experiences a more intensive stillness than after forms of meditation which are consciously aimed at silence.

The stillness that follows weeping is a living, love-filled stillness.

Giving vent to one's feelings in tears has a cathartic and renewing effect. If we cannot give adequate expression to our feelings, we become ill. For the feelings which are suppressed are by no means dead; they then express themselves in neurotic disturbances or in all sorts of addictions. In tears, the unconscious may also find outward expression in feelings. The monastics say that weeping unites the exterior and the interior person, the one living in consciousness, with his or her unconscious. Weeping is a language in which the unknowing can find expressions. Words often fail in expressing the unconscious. In weeping, the unconscious comes into consciousness and can then exert its healing powers. Since disturbing thoughts usually come from the unknowing and can never be understood, if we suppress our unconscious, it also becomes evident from a psychological point of view why weeping draws us into a deeper and more lasting repose than mere relaxing techniques.

In weeping we lay ourselves open to pain and sorrow and allow it to enter into ourselves. Today people try every means to avoid unhappiness and sorrow; they guard themselves against it. It is regarded as a threat to interior peace. Yet this leads

> "inevitably to shallowness of character and impoverishment of life."[63]

The person who is incapable of suffering also becomes incapable of enjoyment.

> "Where there is no suffering, there can be no great joy. Loneliness and emptiness are the results; the next step is looking for a substitute."[64]

One who avoids suffering also becomes incapable of loving. Only those who are willing to take a chance of getting hurt can truly love. In weeping, one lays oneself open to pain, not to take pleasure in it, but to let oneself be touched by it, to receive and to absorb it. Psychology speaks of the labor of grief and regrets, that people have become ever more incapable of grieving.[65] In grieving, pain is activated, integrated, dissolved, and finally healed. Every therapeutic treatment passes through the phase of tears. An analysis will not help patients if it merely reveals to them the cause of their neurosis. The patients can employ this knowledge as a repellent when the actual problem has to be faced. An insight, which I have, avails me nothing; only when it sets itself into me, can it heal me. Without sharing in emotional experience, altering of human behavior is not possible. Not until the pain that has been repressed is allowed to enter into the heart, can one free oneself from the pseudo pain which was employed to shield oneself from the actual suffering. Jung says:

> "Neurosis is always a substitute for real pain."[66]

When a person shies away from proffered suffering he or she plunges into sickness. Healing cannot begin until one surrenders to the repressed pain, the rejected suffering. This surrender is usually accompanied by violent weeping. Weeping relieves us of the pent-up feelings that press outwards. Tears alleviate the pain. We relieve ourselves of suffering by weeping. Weeping offers a last resource to endure a sorrow that threatens to overpower and overwhelm a person, and to respond to it. We know no other response, either in words or in deeds, than to succumb to tears, to relieve ourselves in weeping, to abandon ourselves to the pain and at the same time to relieve it, to rid ourselves of it.

Weeping relieves, mitigates, heals. Tears become all of a sudden freeing, saving, blessed tears. Pain is turned to joy. The person experiences deep within a healing which cannot be threatened by pain – a joy that cannot be touched by disappointment or misfortune. It is the healing power of God, which overcomes all human misery.

Chapter III

PRAYER AND HEALING

Self-knowledge and compunction of heart prepare the ground for the healing of the person. The exposure of the wounds and the relieving of the suppressed pain of themselves have a healing effect. Callousness is given up and the place is indicated where the person must direct his or her efforts at self-healing. Prayer itself is now used as a means to combat evil thoughts and thereby to heal the person. Prayer is for monastics not only analysis, but at the same time therapy. According to the disposition of the one praying, at one time the analytic and at another time the therapeutic element will come to the fore.

Thus far we have considered only the analytic aspect of prayer: self-observation and self-knowledge. Yet at times the analytic aspect seems to be entirely by-passed. Prayer is regarded as pure therapy; it heals a person without having to disclose one's evil thoughts. It is a protection against stirring up the passions.

It appears thus in a Saying of the Ancients:

"Abbot John said: 'I am like a man sitting under a big tree, who sees many wild animals and snakes coming toward him. If he cannot. withstand them, he hastily climbs up the tree and thus saves himself. So it is with me. I sit in my cell and see how evil thoughts press in upon me, and when I am powerless to overcome them, I flee to God in prayer and am thus saved from the evil one."[67]

In a similar way, Cassian sees prayer as protection from evil thoughts which assail a person and draws toward evil. Cassian explains this function of prayer in that the human spirit must out of necessity occupy itself with thoughts. It is up to oneself, therefore, to fill the mind with good thoughts. Through thoughts of God, through meditation, reading and prayer, one can preserve oneself from evil thoughts and so heal the spirit. For, as one thinks of divine matters, evil thoughts will find no place there. But it is not just a matter of place. Thoughts affect the spirit so as to change a person accordingly. By thinking of God a person slowly develops a taste for God and is transformed. Based on this theory, Cassian concludes that prayer is an effective means to change a person interiorly and to bring about healing:

> "It is up to us, in great part, to improve the nature of our thoughts, so that either holy and spiritual thoughts grow in our hearts, or worldly and carnal ones. For this reason, the frequent reading and the constant consideration of Holy Scripture is recommended, so that by this means an opportunity is given us to fill our minds with spiritual content."[68]

Thus we are healed by the godly thoughts to which we give ourselves in prayer. By this means, our thoughts, affections and moods need not be analyzed beforehand. Much more are they healed by what is good. Through the words of Scripture, on which we reflect in prayer, God's Spirit dwells in us: God's holy and at the same time healing Spirit.

In the Sayings of the Ancients, further methods are recommended to us for dealing with our thoughts. Thoughts, in the mind of the Ancients, are allurements and temptations, all that tends to make us interiorly infirm. The proper handling of thoughts is, therefore, a means of healing one's wounds and infirmities. The first method is to turn away resolutely from evil thoughts. Thus says an Ancient:

> "If you do not energetically say to them (your thoughts) 'Get out of here! they will not go away. For, as long as they have peace, they will not depart."[69]

The second method is not to pay any attention at all to evil thoughts, but to take refuge in prayer, to look up to God. Thus Macarius counsels a monastic:

> "If a thought bothers you, do not look down but wholly and entirely up. The Lord will help you instantly."[70]

Another counsels, placing oneself in the presence of God and doing one's best to expel the evil thoughts.[71] The remembrance of the presence of God protects from temptations and heals one who has been wounded by them. God's presence is like an oxygen tent in which the sick person can breathe freely. Enveloped in God's presence, the spirit will be healed.

A third therapeutic method recommended by the Ancients is to stand up and pray at the onset of disturbing thoughts. Bodily movement drives away the thoughts and makes the monastic capable of offering an effective prayer. Oftentimes the bodily movement will be still further extended by going around in one's cell or by making the sign of the cross.

> "It may be that while you are sitting there, your thoughts and the demons press in upon you. If so, get up, go outdoors, say a prayer, walk around your cell, and they will take flight."[72]

The monastics know that it is not necessary for everything within us to be revealed before we can be healed. They rely on the healing power of prayer. One can also become spiritually sound just by praying, if the analysis of thoughts is too burdensome. I do not need to know the exact nature of the infirmity of which I wish to be healed. If I live a healthy life, if I imbibe the healing power of prayer day by day, even my hidden failings will be healed. For prayer unites me to God, the true physician, who knows my wounds far better than I do myself. To devote oneself to prayer is, therefore, the best therapy the monastics recommend to us.

Prayer is regarded by the monastics as a means of healing. But there are different kinds of remedies. The one kind determines the causes of the illness, analyses them, and intensifies them before combating them. Other medicines are like salves that are applied to the wounds without knowing precisely the nature of the wound, or like stimulants which activate the resistance of the person toward different germs not specifically identified.

In the same way, prayer is for the monastics at one time an explorative and analytic means. By self-observation and self-knowledge, the causes of the failings are revealed. At another time prayer is rather a healing balm or stimulant, which can be used to combat all forms of illness without knowing them in particular. By steadfast prayer a person is made interiorly immune to sin and faults. Failings that have sunk in a person are slowly weakened. Such healing often takes place unnoticed and for a long time unknown. Outwardly no change is apparent, yet, interiorly, in the unknowing, a change sets in. Day after day, the farmer cultivates the fields, with no apparent changes. But the plowed field will produce its fruit in due time. So, too, in the unconscious, plowed by prayer, the fruit of conversion develops, though unobserved by many.

For monastics, analytic and therapeutic forms of prayer are not contradictory. Both forms are recommended, according to the condition or the mental capacity of the individual person. Sometimes they are applied in succession, first the therapeutic, and if this does not help, if the unrest and interior confusion persists, the revealing and the analytic. But monastics also know forms of prayer in which the analytic and the therapeutic are combined. The same prayer reveals and heals. A good example of this method of prayer is the Antirheticon of Evagrius. Here the evil thoughts, the spiritual shortcomings, are not simply ignored, inasmuch as they are replaced by thoughts of God. Rather, the thoughts, which according to Evagrius are inspired by demons, are recognized and so-called contra thoughts are opposed to them. Thus monastics, if they feel that they are greedy, should recognize their greediness and combat it with a word from Scripture which will overcome greed.

Evagrius first analyses

> "the thought that refuses to give something to the needy brother or sister, and to the person who asks for a loan, money + Dt. 15:7 f: 'You shall not close your hand to one who is in need. Instead, you shall open your hand and freely give as much as one asks for.'"[73]

When monastics alert themselves to the temptations and repeatedly opposes them with the word of God, the temptations will cease. God's word will prevail over the thought which the demon suggested. It will free the monastics from the vice which tries to hold captive and will heal of the vicious mood, of the unrest which the evil thoughts aroused in them. Thus prayer becomes a wrestling with the ailment. The one who prays clings to God, who heals the infirmity through the constant and meditative word of prayer.

The Sayings of the Ancients recognize similar forms of prayer to overcome temptations to evil thoughts. St. Antony counseled a brother to quietly allow the thoughts to enter his mind. He should not flee from them by imprisoning his body in his cell. If the thoughts then assail him, he should oppose them with words from Holy Scripture. In this way, he will be able to conquer them:

> A brother who was plagued with the urge to leave his cell reported this to Abbot Antony. The sage said to him: "Go and sit down in your cell. Give your body the security of the walls of your cell and do not go outside. Let your thoughts go where they will. Only do not let your body leave your cell. It will suffer; it will not be able to do any work. Finally it will be hungry and mealtime will come which calls you to eat. If hunger says to you shortly before: 'Eat a little bread', reply firmly: 'We do not live by bread alone, but by every word that comes from the mouth of God.' (Dt. 8:2) And he will say: 'Drink a little wine, like Blessed Timothy.' Answer him: 'Call to mind the children of Aminadab, who

observed the order of their father'. (Jer. 35.6) If sleep threatens to overpower you, do not give in to it, for it is written in the Holy Gospel: 'Watch and pray' (Mt. 26: 41), and it is also written: 'They slept and profited not'. (Ps. 75:6) Nourish your soul with the word of God, with watching and prayer, and above all with the constant thought of the Name of our Lord Jesus Christ. Thus you will find the way to overcome bad thoughts."[74]

Another method consists in confronting the thought and analyzing and clarifying it. If it keeps returning, pay no attention to it:

Abbot Poimen said: "If a thought comes to you concerning the urgency of bodily needs and you have put it in order once, and if it returns a second time, and you again have put it in order, and if then it comes back a third time, pay no attention to it, for it is a worthless thought."[75]

Admitting a thought to one's consciousness can go so far that one will act it out in a sort of play. By this means a person finds interior peace:

"I heard an elder say that if his thoughts told him to visit someone, he would get up, take his cloak, go out and walk around his cell. Then he would return and entertain himself with his imaginary guest. In this way he found relief."[76]

Other Ancients make fun of their thoughts. They act as if they were going to carry them out. In this way the menace loses its efficacy:

> "It was said of Abbot Theodore and Abbot Lukios of Ennater, that they made fun of their thoughts for fifty years by saying: 'After this winter we are going to leave this place.' When summer came, they would say: 'After this summer we are going to leave this place.' These unforgettable Fathers always acted in this way."[77]

But for others this method may not be helpful at all. They must employ other means. They must let their thoughts play on a really humorous scene.

> "A brother was besieged by thought: 'You must visit the elder.' But he kept putting it off day after day by saying, 'I will go tomorrow.' For three years, he combated this thought. Finally he said to himself: Imagine that you have gone to see this elder and said to him: 'Is it well with you, Father? For a long time I have desired to see your holiness.' Then he took a basin, washed himself and played the role of the elder: 'You do well in coming, brother. Forgive me, for you have worn yourself out for me. May the Lord reward you!' Then he cooked some food, ate and drank heartily, and immediately the battle was ended."[78]

The methods just cited seem to have nothing to do with prayer. One might better consider them psychological techniques: psychodrama, role-play, and the like. But for monastics, it was clear that they could not heal themselves, that they could not gain the victory over their passions by any technique. The dramatization of a bothersome thought was for them just a somewhat unconventional form of dialogue with God. If conversation with God does not help, because it remains too imaginary, if the analysis of the sources and backgrounds of thoughts is of no avail, then it is possible for many to act out the thoughts before God. Instead of using words, one prays with gestures, with play-acting, and make-believe, to hear the answer from God, an answer that does not consist in a word but in repose and peace and deliverance from the temptation.

Prayer is not a therapeutic means which a monastic can employ like a technique. Prayer heals because it unites us to Christ. Jesus is the real physician who knows how to heal every wound. In prayer we abandon ourselves and our wounds to be healed by him as the physician who was himself wounded on the Cross. In prayer we encounter God's explorative and at the same time healing presence. Because prayer places us in the presence of God and fills us with the spirit of God, it is able to heal. Many Sayings of the Ancients describe this healing function of prayer:

"Persevering prayer improves the spirit in a short time."[79]

"Prayer is a means of warding off sadness and despondency."[80]

"Psalmody quiets the passions and brings the restlessness of the body to repose."[81]

"Prayer produces mildness and goodness."[82]

"Prayer brings forth joy and thanksgiving."[83]

The healing and alleviating power of prayer is praised above all in the writings of Eastern monasticism. The Russian pilgrim relies on the healing power of prayer. Analysis of one's thoughts and the struggle against the evil one with one's own strength only lead to despair. The person is overstrained by it. God has therefore given us prayer as a means for healing:

"Believe me, if you recite this prayer without paying attention to what goes on in your mind, you will soon experience consolation, your anxiety and burdens will disappear, and finally you will be completely calmed, you will become a God-fearing person and all these sinful passions will also disappear."[84]

If people just continue to have recourse to prayer and try to pray without ceasing, all will be well with them, regardless of their own powerlessness to control their passions. Prayer is for the Russian pilgrim the whole purpose of asceticism. The pilgrim gives these simple counsels:

1. Pray, and think about whatever you choose, and your thoughts will be purified by prayer. Prayer will enlighten your spirit, it will drive away unruly thoughts and bring you composure.

2. Pray, and do what you will and your works will be pleasing to God and useful and salutary for yourself.

3. Pray, and do not try by your own strength to overcome your passions. Prayer will bring them to naught.

4. Pray, and fear nothing, neither misfortune nor disaster; prayer will serve you as a shield and will ward off all evil.

5. Pray, in whatever way you choose, but pray always, and do not let yourself be deceived. Be joyful in spirit and at peace. Prayer will achieve everything and will instruct you.[85]

Of course spiritual writers know well that prayer does not excuse one from the duty of putting one's hand to the plow. Prayer and asceticism are not contradictory. They belong together. Without prayer, asceticism tends to self-reliance and one's own achievements. But without asceticism prayer remains empty and irresponsible talk.

Thus says the Philokalia:

"Never forget that prayer by itself is incomplete; it must be combined with all virtues, which are like organs of the soul, and which comprise our inner organism. Not until they are developed to a certain degree are we able to live in the spirit. In the degree in which you acquire them you will also perfect your prayer. Without them prayer produces no fruit."[86]

Prayer leads to

good results only when the person praying guards one's interior and is prepared to combat vices.[87]

Otherwise – so the spiritual writers tell us – one would lose one's mind. To aspire to mysticism without walking the hard way of asceticism is not possible, as they discovered, without injury to one's mental health. If this counsel of the monastics were observed today, we would avoid many psychical injuries which may incur through forms of meditation that promise only happiness and enlightenment, without paying attention to the demands of unsparing self-knowledge and hard work on oneself which are the door to these promises.

61

CONCLUSION

Self-knowledge is not the goal of prayer, but God, whom one desires to encounter and in whose presence one longs to live constantly. Self-knowledge is resented as a psychological preparation. Rather, it comes through prayer itself. While we try to pray well, we so to say, stumble upon ourselves, we get to know ourselves better, and thus become capable of more intensive and purer prayer. By praying we learn to pray. Thus, in seeking help we do not turn first to psychological methods, to place our praying under the standards of psychology.

We rely much more on the purifying and healing power of prayer. Honest prayer, in which we seek not self-satisfaction but an encounter with God, will unsparingly disclose all our faults. It fulfills the function of psychoanalysis without neglecting the religious aspect.

Today we can no longer ignore psychology, and there would be no point in arguing against it. For it has undoubtedly accomplished great things and has been the means of gaining important knowledge about the human person. It has also discovered many ways to help and to heal. Yet, against the background of the psychological care of souls, it would be better today to place greater confidence in the religious way. The Ancients and many who for centuries have followed their counsels have made rich discoveries about the human person, discoveries and knowledge which need not shy away from psychology today. It would be good for us today, to make use of these discoveries, to adopt them through an intensive practice of prayer, and thus be able to experience their salutary effect.

Through repeated prayer monastics have learned who they are, what bad habits, inclinations and moods weaken them interiorly and alienate them from God. Through prayer they have likewise experienced that they are true images of God and that it is important not to allow this image to become blurred or falsified. At the same time they experience again and again that they cannot restore this image of God in themselves by their own efforts, but that only God can heal them.

Only through conversation and with the experience of God's presence, which encompasses us, can we experience God's healing power. The abysses of our interior domain gradually become habitable through prayer. The darkness and demoniacal lose their threat, the weak and frail is healed, moodiness and emotions give way to a relaxed repose and quiet joy. It is not for us to attain self-fulfillment, but God fulfills us by restoring the disfigured image in us.

If we abandon ourselves to God and the healing power in prayer, we will find ourselves, be reconciled and become identical with ourselves, and become whole.

FOOTNOTES

Preliminary Note:

The footnotes were taken from the German edition with some modifications only because it proved impossible to find out the respective English translations. In this way the footnotes hopefully may help those readers interested in verifying the authenticity of the statements in many instances.

[1] Migne, PG (Greek Fathers of the Church) 40, 1267.
[2] Clemens v. Alexandrien, Der Erzieher III, 1. translated by O. Stählin, München, 1934, 134.
[3] PG 79, 536C.
[4] Migne, PL (Latin Fathers of the Church) 494.
[5] PL 183, 571 D.
[6] Apophthegma, 816.
[7] Apophthegma, 4.
[8] Des hl. Augustin Bekenntnisse, introduced by H. Hefele, Jena 1921, 148.
[9] Apophthegma, 546.
[10] Apophthegma, 1125.
[11] PG 79, 1178.

[12] William of St. Thierry, Meditativae Orationes 9, PL 180, 232D-233A.

[13] Ibid., 233 C.

[14] Les sentences des pères du désert, troisiéme recueil (=III), Solesmes, 1976, 147.

[15] Gregory the Great, Dialogue II, 3.

[16] Kleine Philokalie, translated by M. Dietz, Einsiedeln, 1956, 107.

[17] Das immerwährende Herzensgebet. Russische Originaltexte, zusammengestellt und übersetzt von A. Selawry, Weilheim, 1976, 120.

[18] J. Hausheff, Leben aus dem Gebet, Salzburg 1969, 202.

[19] W. Malgo, Gebet u. Erweckung, Pfäffikon, 1972, 16.

[20] Herzensgebet, 102.

[21] Ibid., 117

[22] Compare C. G. Jung, Briefe I, Olten 1972, 418.

[23] Compare C. G. Jung, Gesammelte Werke, Band 9, 1. Halbband, Olten, 1976, 50.

[24] Herzensgebet, 99 f.

[25] Ibid., 101.

[26] Ibid., 50.

[27] PG 40, 1230.

[28] Johannes Cassianus, 24 Unterredungen mit den Vätern, translated by Karl Kohlhund, Kempten, 1879, U 19, 16.

[29] Compare C. G. Jung, Gesammelte Werke, Band 8, Zürich, 1967, 90 ff; Band 9, 1. Halbband, Olten, 1976, 207.

30 Marie-Louise von Franz, Aktive Imagination in der Psychologie von C. G. Jung: Meditation in Religion und Psychotherapie, published by W. Bitter, Stuttgart, 1958, 144.

31 Les sentences III 98; XVI 17.

32 Rule of St. Benedict, Ch. 53.

33 F.M. Dostojewski, Die Brüder Karmasow, Berlin 1950, I 441 f.

34 Rule, Ch. 66.

35 Herzensgebet, 199.

36 Compare the following: J. Hausherr, Penthos. La doctrine de la compone tion dans L'Orient chrétien, Roma, 1944; M. Lot-Borodine, Le mystère du "don des larmes" dans L'Orient chrétien, Supplément á la Vie Spirituelle, 1936.

37 Compare Evagrius Ponticus, Antirhetikon, acedia, 10.

38 PG 79, 1167.

39 Johannes Cassianus, Unterredung 9, 29.

40 Ausgewählte Abhandlungen des Bischofs Isaak von Ninive, translated by G. Bickell, Kempten, 1874, 342.

41 Hausherr, Leben aus dem Gebet, 116.

42 F. M. Dostojewski, Rodion Raskolnikoff, München, 1920, I 37.

43 Compare H. Plessner, Lachen und Weinen. Eine Untersuchung nach den Grenzen menschlichen Verhaltens, Bern, 1950, 89 f, 185 ff.

44 S. P. N. Ephraem Syri Opera Omnia, tom II, Roma, 1740, 347: compare Hausherr, Penthos, 38.

45 André Louf, Reue und Gotteserfahrung.
   Manuskript der Vorbereitungskommission
   des Aebtekongresses, 1972, 3. 22.
46 Johannes Climacus, Die Leiter zum Par-
   adiese, Regensburg, 1874, 139.
47 PL 145, 307-314.
48 PL 147, 309.
49 PG 79, 1183.
50 PG 40, 1270.
51 PL 184, 479.
52 Plessner, Lachen und Weinen, 184.
53 Ibid. 192.
54 Compare Hausherr, Penthos 188.,
55 Compare P. Adnès, Larmes: Dictionnaire de
   Spiritualité, Paris, 1976, Tome IX, 197;
   compare PL 196, 98B.
56 Johannes Cassianus, Unterredung 9, 30.
57 Compare PG 79, 512.
58 Compare same 512 f.
59 Les sentences des pères du désert, nouveau
   recueil (=II), Solosmes 1977, 99 f: N 548.
60 H. Fischle-Carl, Fühlen was Leben ist. Die
   Bedeutung der Gefühlsfunktion, Stuttgart,
   1977, 18.
61 Plessner, Lachen und Weinen, 172.
62 Climacus, 133.
63 Fischle-Carl, 25.
64 Ibid. 25.
65 Compare A. und M. Mitscherlich, Die
   Unfähigkeit zu trauern, München, 1968.
66 C. G. Jung, Gesammelte Werke, Band 11,
   Zürich, 1963, 82.
67 Apophthegma, 327.

[68] Johannes Cassianus, Unterredung 1, 17.
[69] Les sentences II; N 453.
[70] Apophthegma, 456.
[71] Compare Les sentences III, 68; II 15.
[72] Les sentences II, 129; N 592/62.
[73] Evagrius, Antirhetikon, philargyria, 9.
[74] Les sentences III, 141 f; Am 22, 14.
[75] Apophthegma, 614.
[76] Les sentences II, 49; N 394.
[77] Apophthegma, 298.
[78] Les sentences II, 64; N 443.
[79] Apophthegma, 1128.
[80] Apophthegrna, 548.
[81] PG 79, 1186
[82] PG 79, 1170.
[83] PG 79, 1170.
[84] Aufrichtige Erzählungen eines russischen Pilgers, herausgegeben und eingeleitet von E. Jungclausen, Freiburg, 1975, 171.
[85] Ibid., 210.
[86] Herzensgebet ,111.
[87] lbid., 159.

SCHUYLER SPIRITUAL SERIES

Vol. 01 Grün/Scharper, **Benedict of Norcia** Order-No. 10-001
(with The Legacy of Benedict) PB (1992) 108 p. **$ 3.95**

Vol. 02 Ruppert/Grün, **Christ in the Brother** Order-No. 10-002
(According to the Rule of St. Benedict) PB (1992) 61 p. **$ 3.60**

Vol. 03 Clifford Stevens, **Intimacy with God** Order-No. 10-003
(Notes on the Vocation to Celibacy) PB (1992) 120 p. **$ 3.95**

Vol. 04 Clifford Stevens, **The Noblest Love** Order-No. 10-004
(The Sacramentality of Sex in Marriage) PB (1992) 82 p. **$ 3.70**

Vol. 05 Grün, **Dreams on the Spiritual Journey** Order-No. 10-005
PB (1993) 72 p. **$ 4.00**

Vol. 06 Grün, **The Eucharist and Spiritual Growth** Order-No. 10-006
PB (1993) 96 p. **$ 5.00**

Vol. 07 Grün, **Prayer and Self-knowledge** Order-No. 10-007
PB (1993) 72 p. **$ 4.50**

Vol. 08 Grün, **Celibacy - a fullness of life** Order-No. 10-008
PB (1993) 96 p. **$ 5.00**

Vol. 09 Colombás, **Reading God** Order-No. 10-009
(Lectio divina) PB (1993) 144 p. **$ 5.50**

Vol. 10 Grün, **The Challenge of Midlife** Order-No. 10-010
PB (1993) 72 p. **$ 4.50**

Vol. 11 Grün, **The Challenge of Silence** Order-No. 10-011
PB (1993) 72 p. **$ 4.50**

Vol. 12 Grün/Dufner, **Health as a Spiritual Task** Order-No. 10-012
PB (1993) 96 p. **$ 5.00**

Additional Books from BMH-Publications:

Sr. Mary James Uhing, **Windows of a Heart** Order-No. 20-001
(A book of poetry), illustrated. PB (1993) 72 p. **$ 5.00**

The Rosary HC (1988) 400 p. **Order-No. 20-002** **$ 10.00**
153 full color illustrations of the life of Jesus and Mary.

The Holy Mass HC (1993) 448 p. **Order-No. 20-003** **$ 12.00**
(in Word and Picture), 214 full color illustrations.